Season to Taste

QUILTS TO WARM YOUR HOME ALL YEAR LONG

JESSICA DAYON

Martingale®
Create with Confidence

Season to Taste: Quilts to Warm Your Home All Year Long
© 2020 by Jessica Dayon

Martingale®
19021 120th Ave. NE, Ste. 102
Bothell, WA 98011-9511 USA
ShopMartingale.com

Printed in Hong Kong
25 24 23 22 21 20   8 7 6 5 4 3 2 1

Library of Congress Cataloging-in-Publication Data is available upon request.

ISBN: 978-1-68356-111-8

MISSION STATEMENT

We empower makers who use fabric and yarn to make life more enjoyable.

CREDITS

PUBLISHER AND CHIEF VISIONARY OFFICER
Jennifer Erbe Keltner

CONTENT DIRECTOR
Karen Costello Soltys

DESIGN MANAGER
Adrienne Smitke

MANAGING EDITOR
Tina Cook

PRODUCTION MANAGER
Regina Girard

ACQUISITIONS AND DEVELOPMENT EDITOR
Laurie Baker

PHOTOGRAPHERS
Adam Albright
Brent Kane

TECHNICAL EDITOR
Elizabeth Beese

ILLUSTRATOR
Sandy Loi

COPY EDITOR
Melissa Bryan

SPECIAL THANKS
Photography for this book was taken at the homes of:
Karen Burns in Carnation, Washington
Tracie Fish in Kenmore, Washington
Libby Warnken in Ankeny, Iowa

DEDICATION

For my husband, Travis, for endlessly holding my quilts while I tried to get good pictures, and for not asking too many questions when another box of fabric arrived at the door (questions like, Where are you going to fit it? And, Don't you have enough fabric?). Thank you for always encouraging and supporting me. You are my best friend and the best partner I could ask for. I'm lucky to have you by my side forever.

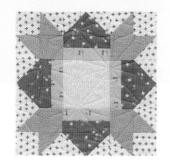

Contents

Introduction

"Live in each season as it passes; breathe the air, drink the drink, taste the fruit, and resign yourself to the influence of the earth."
— HENRY DAVID THOREAU

Since I began making quilts, I have been smitten with the entire process. I love the challenge of designing a quilt and figuring out the exact sizes of pieces I need. I enjoy cutting fabric and then piecing the blocks and quilt top. I get excited to quilt my project or send it out to be quilted. And when I'm ready to bind, I think about the whole process and how I poured my heart into a special creation.

When I first started quilting, each project found a permanent spot in my household. I couldn't imagine tucking a quilt away in a closet until a certain time of year and then pulling it out to enjoy for just a short while. But as I began to accumulate more quilts, it occurred to me that it might be nice to have quilts for each season and holiday. Now I can't imagine not rotating my quilts. Yes, there are some quilts that always stay on a certain bed or wall, but more often than not, I make seasonal quilts and swap out their presence in my house as the calendar changes.

I hope that, like me, you'll look forward to using a special quilt during the season for which it was intended. As the season ends, I enjoy carefully packing up a beloved creation until the time comes to bring it out again. Each year when it's time to switch your quilts with the seasons, take the time to breathe in each season and holiday. I find that I enjoy all of what each season has to offer by displaying the same decorations and quilts, making the same recipes, and repeating traditions year after year. I hope that you find joy in making seasonal quilts and that you spread the joy to other quilters as well.

This book provides three quilt patterns for each season, but for most of the projects, you can alter the seasonal theme by simply changing the fabric colors. In each section you will find a table topper or wall quilt, a throw quilt, and a bed quilt. Some quilts are easy to upsize (or downsize), so feel free to make them in the dimensions that are the most useful to you. My wish is that you discover endless inspiration in these pages to make seasonal quilts for your home and for those you love.

~ Jessica

Posy

The first signs of spring are often subtle hints of changing color across the landscape. In the same way, a mix of fat eighths and fat quarters in subtle colors can bloom into a pretty patchwork array.

FINISHED QUILT: 72½" × 84½"
FINISHED BLOCK: 10" × 10"

Materials

Yardage is based on 42"-wide fabric. Fat quarters are 18" × 21"; fat eighths are 9" × 21".

- 12 fat quarters of assorted pink, yellow, light blue, and green prints for blocks
- 8 fat eighths of assorted pink, yellow, light blue, and green prints for blocks
- 2⅞ yards of white solid for blocks and sashing
- 1 fat quarter of light blue check for cornerstones
- ⅔ yard of yellow floral for inner border
- 1 yard of pink check for outer border
- ¾ yard of green floral for binding
- 6¾ yards of fabric for backing
- 81" × 93" piece of batting

Cutting

All measurements include ¼" seam allowances. Before you begin cutting, separate the 12 fat quarters of assorted prints into groups 1 to 3, with each group containing 4 fat quarters.

From *each* of the group 1 fat quarters, cut:
5 strips, 2½" × 21" (20 total); crosscut *1 strip from each fat quarter* into 8 squares, 2½" × 2½" (32 total; 2 are extra)

From *each* of the group 2 fat quarters, cut:
4 strips, 2½" × 21" (16 total)

From *each* of the group 3 fat quarters, cut:
4 strips, 2½" × 21" (16 total)

From *each* of the fat eighths, cut:
4 strips, 1½" × 21" (32 total)

From the white solid, cut:
5 strips, 10½" × 42"; crosscut into 71 strips, 2½" × 10½"
16 strips, 2½" × 42"; crosscut into 32 strips, 2½" × 21"

From the light blue check, cut:
6 strips, 2½" × 21"; crosscut into 42 squares, 2½" × 2½"

From the yellow floral, cut:
8 strips, 2½" × 42"

From the pink check, cut:
8 strips, 3½" × 42"

From the green floral, cut:
9 strips, 2½" × 42"

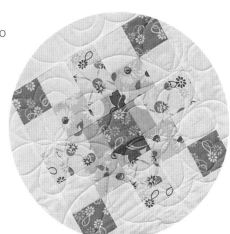

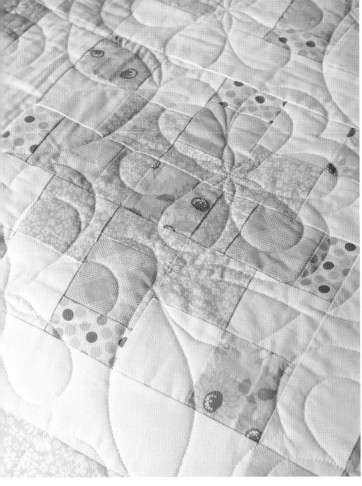

Making the Blocks

Use a ¼" seam allowance. Press all seam allowances in the direction indicated by the arrows.

1 Join a group 1 print 2½" × 21" strip and a white 2½" × 21" strip along the long edges to make strip set A. Repeat to make 16 of strip set A. Crosscut each strip set into eight A segments, 2½" × 4½" (128 segments total).

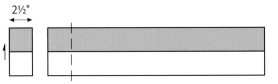

Make 16 of strip set A, 4½" × 21".
Cut each strip set into 8 A segments, 2½" × 4½" (128 total).

2 Using group 2 strips instead of group 1, repeat step 1 to make 16 of strip set B. Crosscut each strip set into eight B segments, 2½" × 4½" (128 segments total).

Make 16 of strip set B, 4½" × 21".
Cut each strip set into 8 B segments, 2½" × 4½" (128 total).

3 Sew an A and a B segment together to make a four-patch unit. The unit should be 4½" square, including seam allowances. Repeat to make 128 four-patch units (32 sets of 4 matching units).

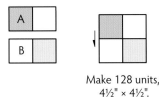

Make 128 units,
4½" × 4½".

4 Join two different fat-eighth 1½" × 21" strips to the long edges of a group 3 print 2½" × 21" strip to make strip set C. Repeat to make 16 of strip set C. Crosscut each strip set into eight C segments, 2½" × 4½" (128 segments total).

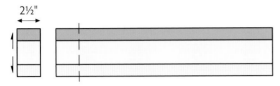

2½"

Make 16 of strip set C, 4½" × 21".
Cut each strip set into 8 C segments, 2½" × 4½" (128 total).

5 Lay out four of the four-patch units, one print 2½" square that matches the A segment in the four-patch units, and four C segments in three horizontal rows as shown. Sew the pieces in each row together, and then join the rows to make the block. The block should measure 10½" square, including seam allowances. Repeat to make 30 blocks. (You will have eight four-patch units and eight C segments left over.)

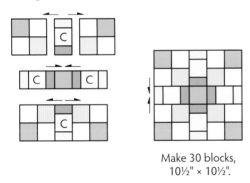

Make 30 blocks,
10½" × 10½".

Assembling the Quilt Top

1 Join six blue check 2½" squares and five white 2½" × 10½" strips to make a sashing row. The row should measure 2½" × 62½", including seam allowances. Repeat to make seven rows.

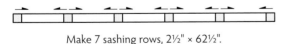

Make 7 sashing rows, 2½" × 62½".

2 Join six white 2½" × 10½" strips and five blocks to make a block row. The row should measure 10½" × 62½", including seam allowances. Repeat to make six rows.

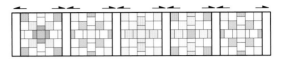

Make 6 block rows, 10½" × 62½".

3 Refer to the quilt assembly diagram to join the sashing rows and block rows in alternating positions. The quilt center should measure 62½" × 74½", including seam allowances.

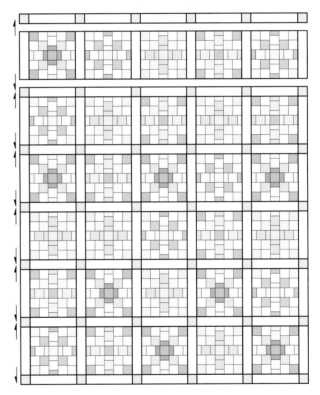

Quilt assembly

4 For the inner border, sew two yellow 2½" × 42" strips together end to end. Repeat to make four pieced strips. Trim two strips to 74½" long. Sew these strips to the sides of the quilt center. Trim the remaining two pieced strips to 66½" long. Sew these strips to the top and bottom edges of the quilt center. The quilt top should now be 66½" × 78½", including seam allowances.

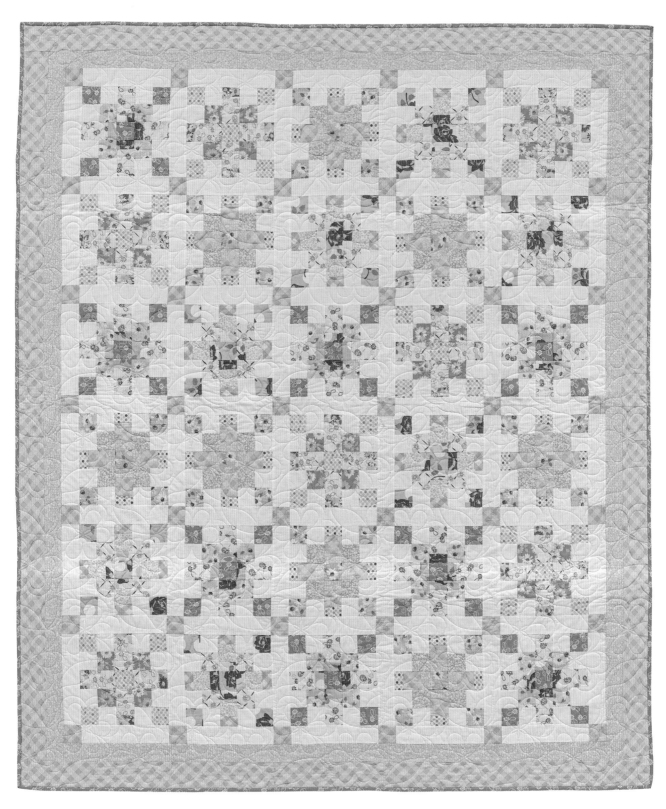

Designed and pieced by Jessica Dayon; machine quilted by David Hurd

5 For the outer border, sew two pink 3½" × 42" strips together end to end. Repeat to make four pieced strips. Trim two strips to 78½" long. Sew these strips to the sides of the quilt center. Trim the remaining two pieced strips to 72½" long. Sew these strips to the top and bottom edges to complete the quilt top, which should measure 72½" × 84½".

Finishing the Quilt

For more details on any finishing steps, visit ShopMartingale.com/HowtoQuilt for free downloadable information.

1 Prepare the quilt backing so that it is about 8" larger in both directions than the quilt top.

2 Layer the quilt top, batting, and backing. Baste the layers together.

3 Hand or machine quilt as desired. The quilt shown is machine quilted with the Forever Flower pantograph design by Apricot Moon.

4 Using the green floral 2½"-wide strips, make the binding and attach it to the quilt.

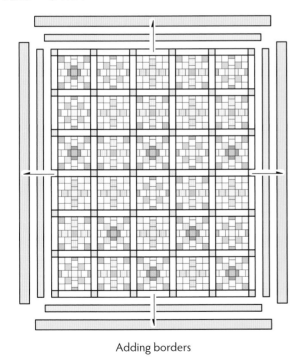

Adding borders

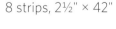

Abloom

Spring is busting out all over! Like the flowers emerging from the earth, these Double Star blocks are exploding with color. Pick your favorite prints and make your blocks bloom!

FINISHED QUILT: 66½" × 66½"
FINISHED BLOCK: 16" × 16"

Materials

Yardage is based on 42"-wide fabric. Fat quarters are 18" × 21"; fat eighths are 9" × 21".

- 16 fat eighths of assorted teal, gold, pink, and green prints for center stars in blocks

- 16 fat quarters of assorted teal, gold, pink, and green prints for outer stars in blocks

- 1⅞ yards of white solid for blocks

- 1 yard of mint green print for blocks and border

- ⅝ yard of aqua print for binding

- 4⅛ yards of fabric for backing

- 73" × 73" piece of batting

Cutting

All measurements include ¼" seam allowances.

From *each* of the fat eighths, cut:
1 square, 4½" × 4½" (16 total)
1 strip, 2⅞" × 21"; crosscut into 4 squares, 2⅞" × 2⅞" (64 total)

From *each* of the fat quarters, cut:
1 square, 9¼" × 9¼" (16 total)
2 squares, 5" × 5" (32 total)

From the white solid, cut:
2 strips, 5¼" × 42"; crosscut into 16 squares, 5¼" × 5¼"
8 strips, 4⅞" × 42"; crosscut into 64 squares, 4⅞" × 4⅞"
4 strips, 2½" × 42"; crosscut into 64 squares, 2½" × 2½"

From the mint green print, cut:
4 strips, 5" × 42"; crosscut into 32 squares, 5" × 5"
8 strips, 1½" × 42"

From the aqua print, cut:
8 strips, 2½" × 42"

Making the Blocks

Use a ¼" seam allowance. Press all seam allowances in the direction indicated by the arrows.

1 Draw a diagonal line from corner to corner on the wrong side of four matching print 2⅞" squares. Layer two marked squares as shown on a white 5¼" square, right sides together. The small squares will overlap in the middle. Sew ¼" from both sides of the line. Cut on the line. Press. Lay a remaining 2⅞" marked square on a triangle piece as shown. Sew ¼" from both sides of the line. Cut apart on the line. Repeat with the remaining triangle piece and 2⅞" marked square. Trim off the dog-ears to complete four flying-geese units. Each should measure 2½" × 4½", including seam allowances. Repeat to make 64 small flying-geese units (16 sets of 4 matching units).

Make 64 units, 2½" × 4½".

2 Arrange four white 2½" squares, four matching small flying-geese units, and one matching print 4½" square in rows as shown. Join the pieces in each row, then join the rows to make a star unit. The unit should be 8½" square, including seam allowances. Repeat to make 16 star units.

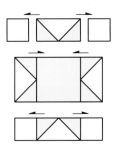 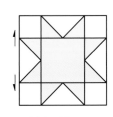

Make 16 units, 8½" × 8½".

Designed and pieced by Jessica Dayon; machine quilted by David Hurd

3 Using a print 9¼" square and four white 4⅞" squares, make four large flying-geese units as shown in step 1 on page 14. Each unit should be 4½" × 8½", including seam allowances. Repeat to make 64 large flying-geese units (16 sets of 4 matching units).

Make 64 units,
4½" × 8½".

4 Draw a diagonal line from corner to corner on the wrong side of a mint green 5" square. Place it, right sides together, on a 5" print square and sew ¼" from both sides of the line. Cut on the line and press. Using a square ruler, line up the 45° line with the diagonal of one half-square-triangle unit and trim the unit to 4½" square. Repeat with the remaining unit. Make 64 half-square-triangle units.

Make 64 units.

5 Arrange the following units into three rows as shown: one star unit, four matching half-square-triangle units, and four large flying-geese units that use the same print as the triangle units. Sew the pieces in each row together, and then join the rows to make a Double Star block. The block should be 16½" square, including seam allowances. Repeat to make 16 blocks.

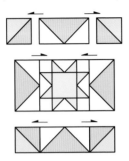
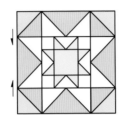

Make 16 blocks,
16½" × 16½".

Assembling the Quilt Top

1 Lay out the blocks in four rows of four blocks each as shown. Rotate every other block 90° so seams nest. Sew the blocks together in each row, and then join the rows. The quilt center should be 64½" square, including seam allowances.

Quilt assembly

2 For the border, sew two mint green 1½" × 42" strips together end to end. Repeat to make four pieced strips. Trim two strips to 64½" long. Sew these strips to the sides of the quilt center. Trim the remaining two pieced strips to 66½" long. Sew these strips to the top and bottom edges to complete the quilt top, which should measure 66½" square.

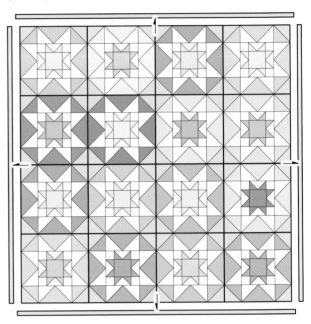

Adding borders

Finishing the Quilt

For more details on any finishing steps, visit ShopMartingale.com/HowtoQuilt for free downloadable information.

1 Prepare the quilt backing so that it is about 6" larger in both directions than the quilt top.

2 Layer the quilt top, batting, and backing. Baste the layers together.

3 Hand or machine quilt as desired. The quilt shown is quilted with the Diamond Chain pantograph design from Leisha Farnsworth.

4 Using the aqua print 2½"-wide strips, make the binding and attach it to the quilt.

Skipping Stones

A bevy of borders and simple units point toward fun. Choose cheery hues to refresh your decor and welcome the promise of bright days and warm weather.

FINISHED QUILT: 45" × 45"
FINISHED BLOCK: 8½" × 8½"

Materials

Yardage is based on 42"-wide fabric. Fat eighths are 9" × 21".

- 6 fat eighths (1 *each* of pink dot, pink geometric, aqua plaid, aqua dot, green narrow stripe, and green wide stripe) for blocks
- 1¾ yards of white solid for blocks and borders 1 and 5
- ¼ yard of pink plaid for border 2
- ¾ yard of aqua stripe for border 3 and binding
- ¼ yard of green dot for border 4
- 2¾ yards of fabric for backing
- 49" × 49" piece of batting

Cutting

All measurements include ¼" seam allowances.

From *each* of the pink dot and aqua plaid, cut:
2 strips, 3½" × 21" (4 total); crosscut into 20 rectangles, 2" × 3½" (40 total)

From the green narrow stripe, cut:
1 strip, 3½" × 21"; crosscut into 5 squares, 3½" × 3½"

From *each* of the pink geometric, aqua dot, and green wide stripe, cut:
2 strips, 3½" × 21" (6 total); crosscut into 16 rectangles, 1½" × 3½" (48 total)

From the white solid, cut:
2 strips, 6" × 42"; crosscut into 9 squares, 6" × 6". Cut each square into quarters diagonally to yield 4 large triangles (36 total).
7 strips, 3½" × 42"; crosscut 4 of the strips into:
    2 strips, 3½" × 39"
    22 squares, 3½" × 3½"; cut 18 of the squares in half diagonally to yield 2 small triangles (36 total)
4 strips, 2½" × 42"; crosscut into:
    2 strips, 2½" × 30"
    2 strips, 2½" × 26"
4 strips, 2" × 42"; crosscut into 80 squares, 2" × 2"

From the pink plaid, cut:
4 strips, 2" × 42"; crosscut into:
    2 strips, 2" × 33"
    2 strips, 2" × 30"

Continued on page 19

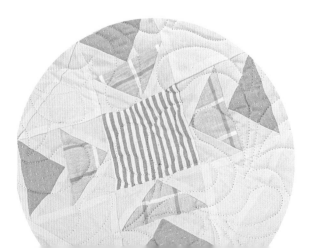

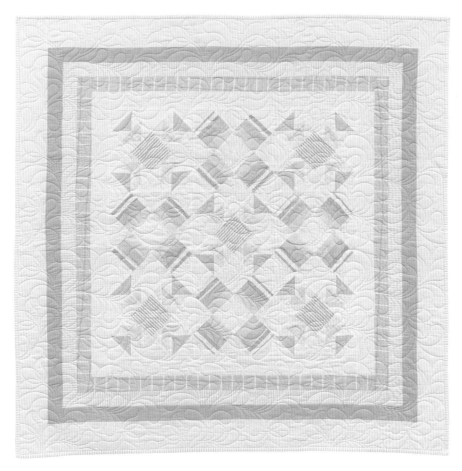

Designed and pieced by Jessica Dayon; machine quilted by David Hurd

Continued from page 17

From the aqua stripe, cut:
5 strips, 2½" × 42"
4 strips, 2" × 42"; crosscut into:
    2 strips, 2" × 36"
    2 strips, 2" × 33"

From the green dot, cut:
4 strips, 2" × 42"; crosscut into:
    2 strips, 2" × 39"
    2 strips, 2" × 36"

Making the Blocks

Use a ¼" seam allowance. Press all seam allowances in the direction indicated by the arrows.

1 Draw a diagonal line from corner to corner on the wrong side of two white 2" squares. Align a square at one end of a pink dot 2" x 3½" rectangle, right sides together, with the line positioned as shown. Sew on the line. Trim, leaving a ¼" seam allowance. Press. Repeat to add the second marked square to the other end of the rectangle. Make 20 pink flying-geese units measuring 2" × 3½".

Make 20 units,
2" × 3½".

4 Lay out four white small triangles, four flying-geese pairs, four white large triangles, and one green narrow stripe 3½" square in diagonal rows as shown. Sew the pieces together in each row, and then join the rows to make block A. Trim the block to 9" square, keeping the design centered. Repeat to make five A blocks.

 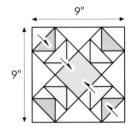

Make 5 A blocks.

5 Sew together one each of green wide stripe, pink geometric, and aqua dot 1½" × 3½" rectangles to make a Rail Fence unit. The unit should be 3½" square, including seam allowances. Repeat to make 16 units.

Make 16 units,
3½" × 3½".

6 Lay out four white small triangles, four Rail Fence units, four white large triangles, and one white 3½" square in diagonal rows as shown. Sew the pieces together in each row, and then join the rows to make block B. Trim the block to 9" square, keeping the design centered. Repeat to make four B blocks.

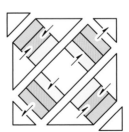 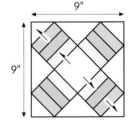

Make 4 B blocks.

2 Using aqua plaid instead of pink dot, repeat step 1 to make 20 aqua flying-geese units.

Make 20 units,
2" × 3½".

3 Sew together one pink and one aqua flying-geese unit to make a flying-geese pair measuring 3½" square, including seam allowances. Make 20 flying-geese pairs.

Make 20 units,
3½" × 3½".

Assembling the Quilt Top

1 Lay out the blocks in three rows of three blocks each, alternating blocks A and B. Join the rows to make the quilt center, which should be 26" square, including seam allowances.

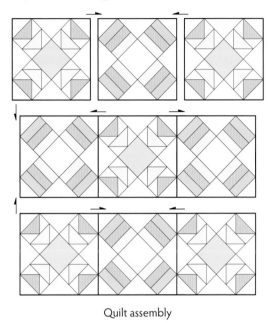

Quilt assembly

2 Sew the white 2½" × 26" strips to the sides of the quilt center. Add the white 2½" × 30" strips to the top and bottom edges. The quilt top should now be 30" square, including seam allowances.

3 Join the pink plaid 2" × 30" strips to the sides of the quilt center. Add the pink plaid 2" × 33" strips to the top and bottom edges. The quilt top should now be 33" square, including seam allowances.

4 Sew the aqua stripe 2" × 33" strips to the sides of the quilt center. Add the aqua stripe 2" × 36" strips to the top and bottom edges. The quilt top should now be 36" square, including seam allowances.

5 Join the green dot 2" × 36" strips to the sides of the quilt center. Add the green dot 2" × 39" strips to the top and bottom edges. The quilt top should now be 39" square, including seam allowances.

6 Sew the white 3½" × 39" strips to the sides of the quilt center. Join the remaining three white 3½" × 42" strips end to end and trim the pieced strip to make two 45"-long strips. Sew these strips to the top and bottom edges to complete the quilt top, which should measure 45" square.

Adding borders

Finishing the Quilt

For more details on any finishing steps, visit ShopMartingale.com/HowtoQuilt for free downloadable information.

1 Prepare the quilt backing so that it is about 4" larger in both directions than the quilt top.

2 Layer the quilt top, batting, and backing. Baste the layers together.

3 Hand or machine quilt as desired. The quilt shown is quilted with the Brenda's Tulips pantograph design from Anne Bright Designs.

4 Using the aqua stripe 2½"-wide strips, make the binding and attach it to the quilt.

Sun-Kissed

One of the most glorious things about summer is the light—early-morning light that wakes you up at the start of a new day, midday light that sets the earth ablaze, and late-evening light that's perfect for sitting on the front porch and watching the children play. Capture all of summer's light in this classic two-color quilt.

FINISHED QUILT: 69½" × 88½"
FINISHED BLOCK: 17" × 17"

Materials

Yardage is based on 42"-wide fabric.

- 5 yards of yellow solid for blocks, cornerstones, middle border, and binding

- 3⅜ yards of white solid for blocks, sashing, and inner and outer borders

- 5½ yards of fabric for backing

- 78" × 97" piece of batting

Cutting

All measurements include ¼" seam allowances.

From the yellow solid, cut:
4 strips, 14" × 42"; crosscut into 12 squares, 14" × 14". Cut each square into quarters diagonally to yield 4 large triangles (48 total).
7 strips, 5¼" × 42"; crosscut into 48 squares, 5¼" × 5¼"
5 strips, 4½" × 42"; crosscut into 36 squares, 4½" × 4½". Cut *24 of the squares* in half diagonally to yield 2 small triangles (48 total).
8 strips, 3½" × 42"
9 strips, 2½" × 42"; crosscut *1 of the strips* into 6 squares, 2½" × 2½"

From the white solid, cut:
15 strips, 2⅞" × 42"; crosscut into 192 squares, 2⅞" × 2⅞"
26 strips, 2½" × 42"; crosscut *9 of the strips* into 17 rectangles, 2½" × 17½"

Designed and pieced by Jessica Dayon; machine quilted by David Hurd

Making the Blocks

Use a ¼" seam allowance. Press all seam allowances in the direction indicated by the arrows.

1 Using a yellow 5¼" square and four white 2⅞" squares, refer to step 1 of "Making the Blocks" on page 14 to make four flying-geese units. Each should be 2½" × 4½", including seam allowances. Repeat to make 192 flying-geese units.

Make 192 units,
2½" × 4½".

2 Sew together four flying-geese units in a row as shown. Make 48 units, each 4½" × 8½", including seam allowances.

Make 48 units,
4½" × 8½".

3 Lay out four yellow small triangles, four yellow large triangles, four units from step 2, and one yellow 4½" square in diagonal rows as shown. Sew the pieces together in each row, and then join the rows to make a block. Trim the block to 17½" square, keeping the design centered. Repeat to make 12 blocks.

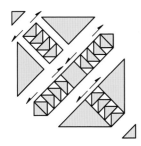
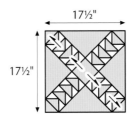

17½"

17½"

Make 12 blocks.

Assembling the Quilt Top

1 Join three white 2½" × 17½" rectangles and two yellow 2½" squares to make a sashing row. The row should be 2½" × 55½", including seam allowances. Repeat to make three rows.

Make 3 sashing rows, 2½" × 55½".

2 Join three blocks and two white 2½" × 17½" rectangles to make a block row. The row should be 17½" × 55½", including seam allowances. Repeat to make four rows.

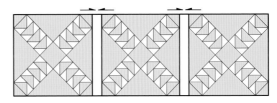

Make 4 block rows, 17½" × 55½".

3 Join the sashing and block rows together, alternating them as shown in the quilt assembly diagram on page 26. The quilt center should be 55½" × 74½", including seam allowances.

4 For the inner border, sew two white 2½" × 42" strips together end to end. Repeat to make four pieced strips. Trim two strips to 55½" long and sew these strips to the top and bottom edges of the quilt center. Trim the remaining pieced strips to 78½" long and sew these strips to the sides of the quilt center. The quilt top should now be 59½" × 78½", including seam allowances.

5 For the middle border, sew the eight yellow 3½" × 42" strips together end to end. Trim the pieced strip to make two strips 84½" long and two strips 59½" long. Sew the 59½"-long strips to the top and bottom edges of the quilt top. Sew the 84½"-long strips to the sides. The quilt top should now be 65½" × 84½", including seam allowances.

6 For the outer border, sew the remaining white 2½" × 42" strips together end to end. Trim the pieced strip to make two strips 88½" long and two strips 65½" long. Sew the 65½"-long strips to the top and bottom edges of the quilt top. Sew the 88½"-long strips to the sides to complete the quilt top, which should measure 69½" × 88½".

Finishing the Quilt

For more details on any finishing steps, visit ShopMartingale.com/HowtoQuilt for free downloadable information.

1 Prepare the quilt backing so that it is about 8" larger in both directions than the quilt top.

2 Layer the quilt top, batting, and backing. Baste the layers together.

3 Hand or machine quilt as desired. The quilt shown is quilted with the Rind pantograph design from Piece N Quilt.

4 Using the yellow 2½"-wide strips, make the binding and attach it to the quilt.

Quilt assembly

Steadfast

Celebrate the season with stars and stripes that set the tone for summertime fun and picnics aplenty. Steadfast is perfect for precut fat eighths and fat quarters, and picking your assortment of prints is part of the fun in making this sparkler!

FINISHED QUILT: 48½" × 48½"
FINISHED BLOCK: 20" × 20"

Materials

Yardage is based on 42"-wide fabric. Fat quarters are 18" × 21"; fat eighths are 9" × 21".

- 11 fat quarters of assorted cream prints for stripe blocks and border
- 7 fat eighths of assorted red prints for stripe blocks
- 9 fat eighths of assorted navy prints for border
- ½ yard of navy tone on tone for binding
- 3 yards of fabric for backing
- 53" × 53" piece of batting

Cutting

All measurements include ¼" seam allowances.

From *each* cream print fat quarter, cut:
3 strips, 2½" × 21" (33 total; 2 are extra); crosscut *1 of the strips* into 4 squares, 2½" × 2½" (44 total)
3 strips, 1½" × 21"; crosscut into 32 squares, 1½" × 1½" (352 total)

From *each* red print fat eighth, cut:
3 strips, 2½" × 21" (21 total; 1 is extra)

From *each* navy print fat eighth, cut:
2 strips, 2½" × 21" (18 total); crosscut into 20 rectangles, 1½" × 2½" (180 total; 4 are extra)
2 strips, 1½" × 21" (18 total); crosscut into 20 squares, 1½" × 1½" (180 total; 4 are extra)

From the navy tone on tone, cut:
6 strips, 2½" × 42"

Making the Blocks

Use a ¼" seam allowance. Press all seam allowances in the direction indicated by the arrows.

1 Sew together five assorted red and five assorted cream 2½" × 21" strips in alternating positions. To reduce the chance of your finished block being bowed, alternate the sewing direction as you add each strip, but try to keep one end of your strip set as even as possible. Don't worry if the other end of the strip set doesn't line up. Once the strips are sewn together, trim the block to 20½" square. Repeat to make four stripe blocks.

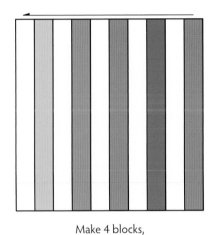

Make 4 blocks,
20½" × 20½".

2 Draw a diagonal line from corner to corner on the wrong side of two cream 1½" squares. Align a square at one end of a navy 1½" x 2½" rectangle, right sides together, with the line positioned as shown. Sew on the line. Trim, leaving a ¼" seam allowance. Press. Repeat to add the second marked square to the other end of the rectangle. Make four matching flying-geese units measuring 1½" x 2½". Repeat to make 176 flying-geese units total (44 sets of 4 matching units).

Make 176 units,
1½" × 2½".

3 Matching the prints used in the flying-geese units, arrange four flying-geese units, one cream 2½" square, and four navy 1½" squares in three rows as shown. Sew the pieces in each row together, and then join the rows to make a Star block. The block should be 4½" square, including seam allowances. Repeat to make 44 Star blocks for the border.

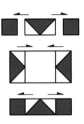

Make 44 blocks,
4½" × 4½".

Assembling the Quilt Top

1 Sew together the stripe blocks in two rows of two blocks each, paying close attention to the orientation of the blocks in the quilt assembly diagram. Join the rows to make the quilt center. The quilt center should be 40½" square, including seam allowances.

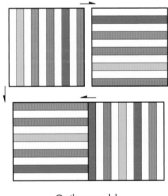

Quilt assembly

2 Sew together 10 Star blocks to make a short border strip that measures 4½" × 40½", including seam allowances. Repeat to make two short borders.

Make 2 short borders, 4½" × 40½".

Designed and pieced by Jessica Dayon; machine quilted by David Hurd

3 Sew together 12 Star blocks to make a long border strip that measures 4½" × 48½", including seam allowances. Repeat to make two long borders.

Make 2 long borders, 4½" × 48½".

4 Sew the short border strips to the sides of the quilt center. Sew the long border strips to the top and bottom edges to complete the quilt top, which should measure 48½" square.

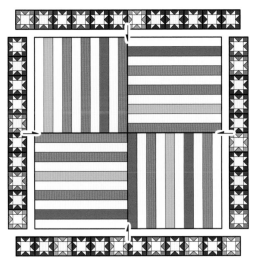

Adding borders

Finishing the Quilt

For more details on any finishing steps, visit ShopMartingale.com/HowtoQuilt for free downloadable information.

1 Prepare the quilt backing so that it is about 4" larger in both directions than the quilt top.

2 Layer the quilt top, batting, and backing. Baste the layers together.

3 Hand or machine quilt as desired. The quilt shown is quilted with the Stars and Loops pantograph design by Linda V. Taylor.

4 Using the navy tone-on-tone 2½"-wide strips, make the binding and attach it to the quilt.

Backyard

Everyone needs a summertime picnic quilt on hand. While any old blanket might be good enough to spread out for lunch at the park, lie on at the beach, or snuggle under for some nighttime stargazing, a handmade quilt is made with the love on which memories are built. As a bonus, this one is big enough for sharing!

FINISHED QUILT: 57½" × 71½"
FINISHED BLOCK: 12" × 12"

Materials

Yardage is based on 42"-wide fabric. Fat quarters are 18" × 21"; fat eighths are 9" × 21".

- ⅝ yard of green print for blocks
- 1½ yards of white-and-blue print for block backgrounds and inner border
- 4 fat quarters (1 *each* of aqua, pink, red, and navy prints) for blocks
- 4 fat eighths (1 *each* of pink, red, taupe, and aqua prints) for blocks
- ½ yard of yellow print for block centers
- ⅞ yard of white floral for sashing
- ¾ yard of navy diagonal plaid for cornerstones and binding
- ⅜ yard of butterscotch print for middle border
- ¾ yard of red floral for outer border
- 3⅝ yards of fabric for backing
- 64" × 78" piece of batting

Cutting

All measurements include ¼" seam allowances.

From the green print, cut:
2 strips, 5¾" × 42"; crosscut into 12 squares, 5¾" × 5¾"
3 strips, 2½" × 42"; crosscut into 48 squares, 2½" × 2½"

From the white-and-blue print, cut:
2 strips, 5¾" × 42"; crosscut into 12 squares, 5¾" × 5¾"
14 strips, 2½" × 42"; crosscut 9 of the strips into 144 squares, 2½" × 2½"

From *each* print fat quarter, cut:
3 strips, 4½" × 21" (12 total); crosscut into:
    12 rectangles, 2½" × 4½" (48 total)
    12 strips, 1½" × 4½" (48 total)

From *each* print fat eighth, cut:
1 strip, 4½" × 21" (4 total); crosscut into 12 strips, 1½" × 4½" (48 total)

From the yellow print, cut:
3 strips, 4½" × 21; crosscut into 12 squares, 4½" × 4½"

From the white floral, cut:
2 strips, 12½" × 42"; crosscut into 31 strips, 2½" × 12½"

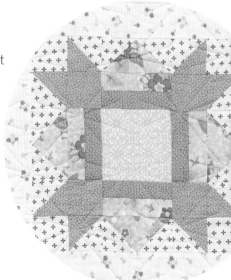

Continued on page 34

Continued from page 33

From the navy diagonal plaid, cut:

9 strips, 2½" × 42"; crosscut *2 of the strips* into 20
    squares, 2½" × 2½"*

From the butterscotch print, cut:

6 strips, 2" × 42"

From the red floral, cut:

7 strips, 3½" × 42"

*If your plaid is not printed on the diagonal but you
want the same look, cut the strips on the bias instead
of on the crosswise grain.*

Making the Blocks

Use a ¼" seam allowance. Press all seam
allowances in the direction indicated by the arrows.

1 On the wrong side of a green 5¾" square,
draw a diagonal line from corner to corner in
both directions. Place the marked square, right sides
together, on a white-and-blue 5¾" square. Sew ¼"
from both sides of each of the two lines.

2 Cut along the lines, and then cut across the
square at the vertical and horizontal
midpoints to make eight half-square triangle units.

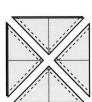

3 Repeat steps 1 and 2 to make 96 half-square-
triangle units. Trim each half-square-triangle
unit to 2½" square, including seam allowances.

Make 96 units.

4 Sew together one white-and-blue 2½"
square, two half-square-triangle units, and
one green 2½" square in two rows as shown. Join
the rows to make a leaf unit. The unit should be 4½"
square, including seam allowances. Repeat to make
48 leaf units.

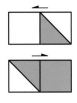

Make 48 units,
4½" × 4½".

5 Draw a diagonal line from corner to corner on
the wrong side of two white 2½" squares.
Align a square at one end of a print 2½" x 4½"
rectangle, right sides together, with the line
positioned as shown. Sew on the line. Trim, leaving a
¼" seam allowance. Press. Repeat to add the second
marked square to the other end of the rectangle.
Make 12 matching flying-geese units measuring
2½" x 4½", including seam allowances. Repeat to
make 48 flying-geese units (four sets of 12).

Make 48 units,
2½" × 4½".

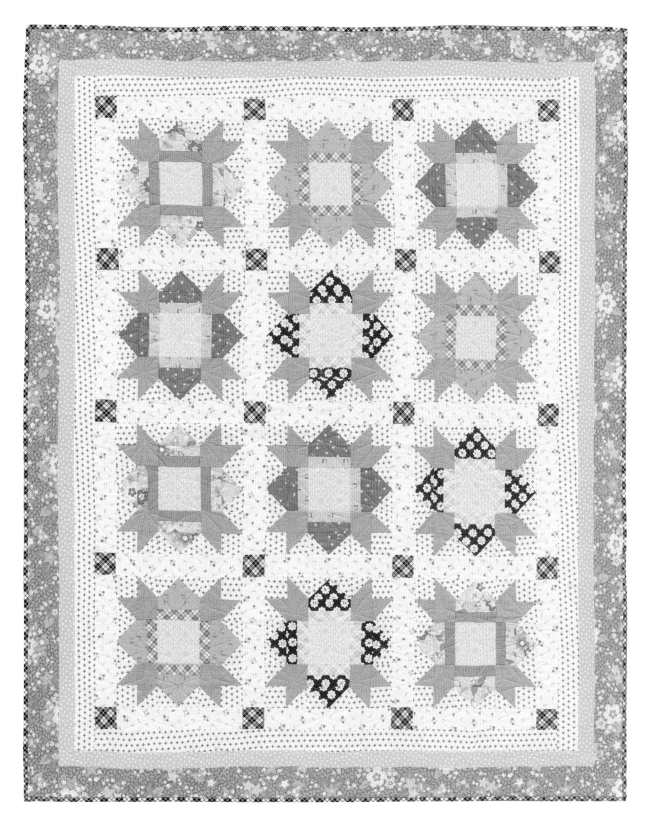

Designed and pieced by Jessica Dayon; machine quilted by David Hurd

6 Sew together a 1½" × 4½" strip cut from a fat quarter and a 1½" × 4½" strip cut from a fat eighth as shown to make a side unit. The unit should be 2½" × 4½", including seam allowances. Make 12 matching side units. Repeat to make 48 side units (four sets of 12).

Make 48 units,
2½" × 4½".

7 Matching the pieces that were cut from a fat quarter, sew together a flying-geese unit and a side unit to make a petal unit. The unit should be 4½" square, including seam allowances. Make 12 matching petal units. Repeat to make 48 petal units (four sets of 12).

Make 48 units,
4½" × 4½".

8 Lay out four leaf units, four matching petal units, and one yellow 4½" square in three rows as shown. Sew the pieces in each row together, and then join the rows to make a block. The block should be 12½" square, including seam allowances. Repeat to make 12 blocks.

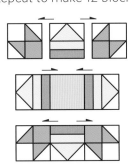 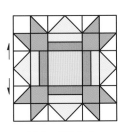

Make 12 blocks,
12½" × 12½".

Assembling the Quilt Top

1 Join four navy 2½" squares and three white floral 2½" × 12½" strips to make a sashing row. The row should be 2½" × 44½", including seam allowances. Repeat to make five rows.

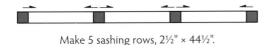

Make 5 sashing rows, 2½" × 44½".

2 Join four white floral 2½" × 12½" strips and three blocks to make a block row. The row should be 12½" × 44½", including seam allowances. Repeat to make four rows.

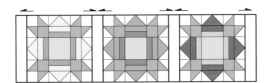

Make 4 block rows, 12½" × 44½".

3 Join the sashing rows and block rows, alternating them as shown in the quilt assembly diagram at right. The quilt center should be 44½" × 58½", including seam allowances.

4 For the inner border, sew the white-and-blue 2½" × 42" strips together end to end. Trim the pieced strip to make two strips 62½" long and two strips 44½" long. Sew the 44½"-long strips to the top and bottom edges of the quilt top. Sew the 62½"-long strips to the sides. The quilt top should now be 48½" × 62½", including seam allowances.

5 For the middle border, sew the butterscotch 2" × 42" strips together end to end. Trim the pieced strip to make two strips 65½" long and two strips 48½" long. Sew the 48½"-long strips to the top and bottom edges of the quilt top. Sew the 65½"-long strips to the sides. The quilt top should now be 51½" × 65½", including seam allowances.

6 For the outer border, sew the red floral 3½" × 42" strips together end to end. Trim the pieced strip to make two strips 71½" long and

two strips 51½" long. Sew the 51½"-long strips to the top and bottom edges of the quilt top. Sew the 71½"-long strips to the sides to complete the quilt top, which should measure 57½" × 71½".

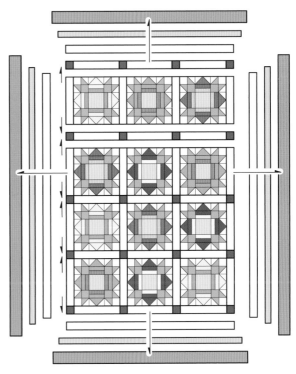

Quilt assembly

Finishing the Quilt

For more details on any finishing steps, visit ShopMartingale.com/HowtoQuilt for free downloadable information.

1 Prepare the quilt backing so that it is about 6" larger in both directions than the quilt top.

2 Layer the quilt top, batting, and backing. Baste the layers together.

3 Hand or machine quilt as desired. The quilt shown is machine quilted with the Sashiko pantograph design by Karen Thompson from Intelligent Quilting.

4 Using the navy plaid 2½"-wide strips, make the binding and attach it to the quilt.

Gratitude

Did you know that research has shown gratitude can have many positive effects on our lives, including improved physical and mental health? Give yourself a daily reminder to seek out the good by embroidering a simple phrase of thankfulness on this beautiful fall leaf quilt.

FINISHED QUILT: 54½" × 54½"
FINISHED BLOCKS: 9" × 9" and 18" × 18"

Materials

Yardage is based on 42"-wide flannel. Fat quarters are 18" × 21"; fat eighths are 9" × 21"; fat sixteenths are 9" × 10½".

- 32 fat sixteenths of assorted brown, red, orange, tan, navy, and green prints (referred to collectively as "dark") for small Leaf blocks
- 32 fat eighths of assorted light prints for small Leaf blocks
- 1 fat quarter of orange print for large Leaf block
- 1 fat quarter of cream tone on tone for large Leaf block
- ½ yard of dark green print for binding
- 3½ yards of fabric for backing
- 61" × 61" piece of batting
- 1 skein of brown embroidery floss, removable fabric marker, and embroidery needle (size 7 or 9) for embroidery (optional)

Cutting

All measurements include ¼" seam allowances.

From *each* assorted dark fat sixteenth, cut:
1 square, 6" × 6" (32 total)
1 square, 4" × 4" (32 total); cut each square in half diagonally to yield 2 triangles (64 total)
1 square, 3½" × 3½" (32 total)

From *each* assorted light fat eighth, cut:
1 square, 6" × 6" (32 total)
3 squares, 3½" × 3½" (96 total)
1 strip, 1½" × 5" (32 total)

From the orange print, cut:
1 square, 10" × 10"
1 square, 7" × 7"; cut the square in half diagonally to yield 2 triangles
1 square, 6½" × 6½"

From the cream tone on tone, cut:
1 square, 10" × 10"
1 strip, 6½" × 21"; crosscut into 3 squares, 6½" × 6½"
1 strip, 2" × 10½"

From the dark green print, cut:
6 strips, 2½" × 42"

Making the Blocks

Use a ¼" seam allowance. Press all seam allowances in the direction indicated by the arrows.

1 Layer one dark and one light 6" square right sides together and sew around the perimeter, ¼" from the edge. Cut the square into quarters diagonally. Press. Trim each of the four half-square-triangle units to 3½" square, including seam allowances. Repeat to make 128 small half-square-triangle units (32 sets of four matching units).

 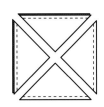 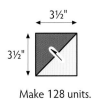

Make 128 units.

2 Using the same light and dark print as in one set from step 1, sew two dark triangles to opposite sides of a light 1½" × 5" strip as shown. To trim, line up the 45° line of a ruler on the middle of the light strip as shown. Trim the excess. Rotate the unit 180°. Line up the left and bottom edges of the unit with the 3½" lines of the ruler. Trim the excess. The small stem unit should be 3½" square, including seam allowances. Repeat to make 32 small stem units.

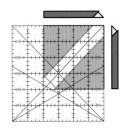

Make 32 units.

3 Using matching light and dark prints, arrange four small half-square-triangle units, one dark 3½" square, three matching light 3½" squares, and one small stem unit in three horizontal rows as shown. Sew the pieces in each row together, and then join the rows to make a small Leaf block. The block should be 9½" square, including seam allowances. Repeat to make 32 small Leaf blocks.

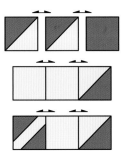 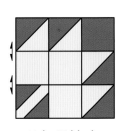

Make 32 blocks,
9½" × 9½".

4 Using the cream and orange 10" squares, refer to step 1 to make four large half-square-triangle units. Trim each unit to 6½" square, including seam allowances.

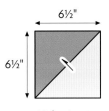

Make 4 units.

5 Sew the two orange triangles to opposite sides of the cream 2" × 10½" strip as shown. In the same manner as for the small stem unit, center and trim the large stem unit to be 6½" square, including seam allowances.

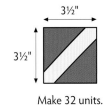 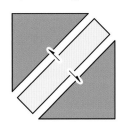

Make 1 unit.

6 Using the four large half-square-triangle units, the orange 6½" square, the cream 6½" squares, and the large stem unit, repeat step 3 to make a large Leaf block. The block should be 18½" square, including seam allowances.

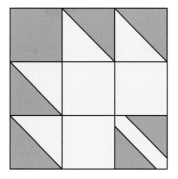

Make 1 block,
18½" × 18½".

7 To embroider the large Leaf block with the phrase *There Is Always Something to Be Grateful For,* download the free pattern at ShopMartingale.com/SeasontoTaste. Using the embroidery pattern with a light box or sunny window, trace the words onto the center of the large leaf with the removable fabric marker. Embroider the words, using a backstitch for the thin letters and a padded satin stitch for the thick letters.

3 1 2

Backstitch

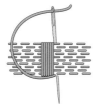

Padded satin stitch
(Stitch along outline with running stitch,
fill in with running stitch,
then satin stitch over top.)

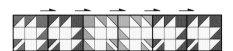

Designed and pieced by Jessica Dayon; quilted by Teresa Silva

Assembling the Quilt Top

1 Join six small Leaf blocks as shown to make row A. The row should be 9½" × 54½", including seam allowances. Make two of row A.

Row A. Make 2, 9½" × 54½".

2 Join six small Leaf blocks as shown to make row B. The row should be 9½" × 54½", including seam allowances. Make two of row B.

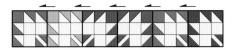

Row B. Make 2, 9½" × 54½".

3 To make row C, lay out six small Leaf blocks in two horizontal rows on the left side of the large Leaf block, and place two small Leaf blocks in a vertical row on the right as shown. First sew together the small Leaf blocks in each row. Join the horizontal rows, and then sew them to the left of the large Leaf block. Sew the vertical row to the right side of the large Leaf block to make row C. The row should be 18½" × 54½", including seam allowances.

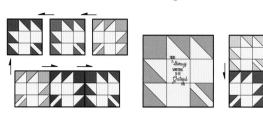

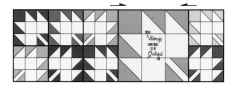

Row C. Make 1, 18½" × 54½".

4 Join the block rows as shown in the quilt assembly diagram below to complete the quilt top, which should measure 54½" square.

Finishing the Quilt

For more details on any finishing steps, visit ShopMartingale.com/HowtoQuilt for free downloadable information.

1 Prepare the quilt backing so that it is about 6" larger in both directions than the quilt top.

2 Layer the quilt top, batting, and backing. Baste the layers together.

3 Hand or machine quilt as desired. The quilt shown here is custom machine quilted with an echoing spiral in each leaf. The assorted print block backgrounds were stitched with a square spiral in the squares and a boomerang shape in the triangles.

4 Using the dark green 2½"-wide strips, make the binding and attach it to the quilt.

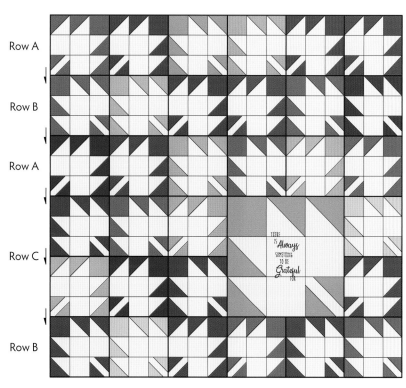

Quilt assembly

Harvest

Gather the warm, welcoming hues of autumn and turn them into a quilt you're guaranteed to "fall" in love with. Strip piecing makes this one-block design go together quickly, so you'll have plenty of time to enjoy the fruits of your labor.

FINISHED QUILT: 66½" × 86½"
FINISHED BLOCK: 8" × 8"

Materials

Yardage is based on 42"-wide fabric. Fat quarters are 18" × 21"; fat eighths are 9" × 21".

- ⅝ yard of brown stripe for blocks and cornerstones
- 1 yard of brown floral for blocks
- ⅞ yard of white floral A for blocks
- 1 yard of white floral B for blocks
- 1 yard of orange print for blocks
- 1 ⅝ yards of yellow solid for sashing
- 1⅛ yards of yellow floral for border
- ¾ yard of brown print for binding
- 5⅓ yards of fabric for backing
- 75" × 95" piece of batting

Cutting

All measurements include ¼" seam allowances.

From the brown stripe, cut:
2 strips, 5" × 42"; crosscut into 14 squares, 5" × 5"
3 strips, 2½" × 42"; crosscut into 35 squares, 2½" × 2½"

From the brown floral, cut:
6 strips, 5" × 42"; crosscut into 48 squares, 5" × 5"

From white floral A, cut:
5 strips, 5" × 42"; crosscut into 34 squares, 5" × 5"

From white floral B, cut:
12 strips, 2½" × 42"

From the orange print, cut:
13 strips, 2½" × 42"

From the yellow solid, cut:
6 strips, 8½" × 42"; crosscut into 82 rectangles, 2½" × 8½"

From the yellow floral, cut:
8 strips, 4½" × 42"

From the brown print, cut:
9 strips, 2½" × 42"

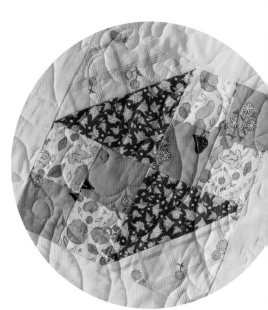

Making the Blocks

Use a ¼" seam allowance. Press all seam allowances in the direction indicated by the arrows.

1 Draw a diagonal line from corner to corner on the wrong side of a brown floral 5" square. Place it, right sides together, on a 5" brown stripe square and sew ¼" from both sides of the marked line. Cut on the line and press. Using a square ruler, line up the 45° line with the diagonal of the half-square-triangle unit and trim the unit to 4½" square. Repeat with the remaining unit. Repeat to make 28 half-square-triangle units.

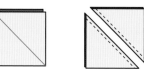

Make 28 units.

2 Using a brown floral and a white floral A 5" square, repeat step 1 to make 68 half-square-triangle units.

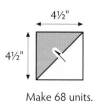

Make 68 units.

3 Sew together one orange print and one white floral B 2½" × 42" strip to make a strip set. Make 12 strip sets measuring 4½" × 42". Crosscut the strip sets into 192 segments, 2½" wide.

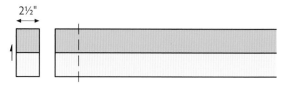

Make 12 strip sets, 4½" × 42".
Cut 192 segments, 2½" × 4½".

4 Join two step 3 segments to make a four-patch unit. The unit should be 4½" square, including seam allowances. Repeat to make 96 four-patch units.

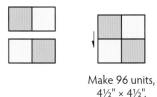

Make 96 units,
4½" × 4½".

5 Arrange two half-square-triangle units from step 1 and two four-patch units in two rows as shown. Sew together the pieces in each row, and then join the rows to make a corner block. The block should be 8½" square, including seam allowances. Make four corner blocks.

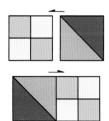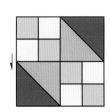

Make 4 corner blocks,
8½" × 8½".

6 Using one half-square-triangle unit from step 1 and one half-square-triangle unit from step 2, repeat step 5 to make an edge block. Make 20 edge blocks.

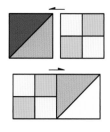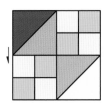

Make 20 edge blocks,
8½" × 8½".

7 Using two half-square-triangle units from step 2, repeat step 5 to make an inner block. Make 24 inner blocks.

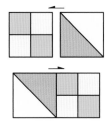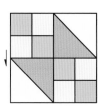

Make 24 inner blocks,
8½" × 8½".

Assembling the Quilt Top

1 Join five brown stripe 2½" squares and six yellow solid 2½" × 8½" rectangles to make a sashing row. The row should be 2½" × 58½", including seam allowances. Repeat to make seven sashing rows.

Make 7 sashing rows, 2½" × 58½".

2 Referring to the diagram, sew together two corner blocks, five yellow solid 2½" × 8½" rectangles, and four edge blocks to make an end block row. The row should be 8½" × 58½", including seam allowances. Make two end block rows.

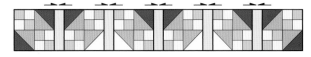

Make 2 end block rows, 8½" × 58½".

3 Sew together two edge blocks, five yellow solid 2½" × 8½" rectangles, and four inner blocks as shown to make a center block row. The row should be 8½" × 58½", including seam allowances. Make six center block rows.

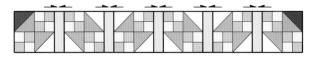

Make 6 center block rows, 8½" × 58½".

Designed and pieced by Jessica Dayon; machine quilted by David Hurd

④ Join the sashing rows and block rows, alternating them as shown in the quilt assembly diagram below. The quilt center should be 58½" × 78½", including seam allowances.

⑤ For the border, sew the yellow floral 4½" × 42" strips together end to end. Trim the pieced strip to make two strips 86½" long and two strips 58½" long. Sew the 58½"-long strips to the top and bottom edges of the quilt top. Sew the 86½"-long strips to the sides to complete the quilt top, which should measure 66½" × 86½".

Finishing the Quilt

For more details on any finishing steps, visit ShopMartingale.com/HowtoQuilt for free downloadable information.

① Prepare the quilt backing so that it is about 8" larger in both directions than the quilt top.

② Layer the quilt top, batting, and backing. Baste the layers together.

③ Hand or machine quilt as desired. The quilt shown is machine quilted with a leaf design.

④ Using the brown print 2½"-wide strips, make the binding and attach it to the quilt.

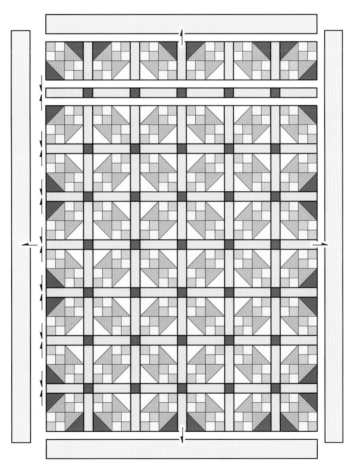

Quilt assembly

Spooky

No boos, no frights, just a quilting delight is what you'll create when you take advantage of the magical combination of orange and black. Use assorted values of these two popular Halloween colors with a range of subdued background prints to make your quilt spook-tacular!

FINISHED QUILT: 70½" × 94½"
FINISHED BLOCK: 12" × 12"

Materials

Yardage is based on 42"-wide fabric. Fat quarters are 18" × 21".

- ½ yard of black floral print for block centers
- ½ yard of black leaf print for block centers
- 2 yards of cream print for blocks
- ⅝ yard *each* of 6 assorted orange prints for blocks
- 6 fat quarters of assorted gray prints for blocks
- 3 fat quarters of assorted light prints for blocks
- 1⅛ yards of dark gray print for blocks and inner border
- ⅞ yard of orange floral for outer border
- ¾ yard of black chevron print for binding
- 5¾ yards of fabric for backing
- 79" × 103" piece of batting

Cutting

All measurements include ¼" seam allowances.

From the black floral, cut:
3 strips, 4½" × 42"; crosscut into 18 squares, 4½" × 4½"

From the black leaf print, cut:
3 strips, 4½" × 42"; crosscut into 17 squares, 4½" × 4½"

From the cream print, cut:
6 strips, 5" × 42"; crosscut into 48 squares, 5" × 5". Cut each square in half diagonally to yield 2 triangles (96 total).
14 strips, 2½" × 42"; crosscut into 216 squares, 2½" × 2½"

From *each* assorted orange print, cut:
1 strip, 5" × 42" (6 total); crosscut into 6 squares, 5" × 5". Cut each square in half diagonally to yield 2 triangles (72 total; 4 will be extra).
3 strips, 4½" × 42"; crosscut into:
  12 squares, 4½" × 4½" (72 total)
  12 rectangles, 2½" × 4½" (72 total; 4 will be extra)

From *each* gray print fat quarter, cut:
2 strips, 5" × 21" (12 total); crosscut into 6 squares, 5" × 5". Cut each square in half diagonally to yield 2 triangles (72 total).
2 strips, 2½" × 21" (12 total); crosscut into 24 squares, 2½" × 2½" (144 total)

From *each* light print fat quarter, cut:
3 strips, 4½" × 21" (9 total); crosscut into 24 rectangles, 2½" × 4½" (72 total; 4 will be extra)

Continued on page 52

Continued from page 51

From the dark gray print, cut:

3 strips, 5" × 42"; crosscut into 22 squares, 5" × 5". Cut each square in half diagonally to yield 2 triangles (44 total).

8 strips, 2½" × 42"

From the orange floral, cut:

8 strips, 3½" × 42"

From the black chevron print, cut:

9 strips, 2½" × 42"

Making Blocks A, B, and C

Use a ¼" seam allowance. Press all seam allowances in the direction indicated by the arrows.

1 Draw a diagonal line from corner to corner on the wrong side of four cream 2½" squares. Align one 2½" square, right sides together, with a corner of a black floral 4½" square. Sew on the diagonal line. Cut ¼" from the stitching line. Press. Repeat with the other squares at the remaining corners to make a center unit. The center unit should be 4½" square, including seam allowances. Make 18 center units.

Make 18 center units,
4½" × 4½".

2 Using an orange 4½" square, two matching gray 2½" squares, and two cream 2½" squares, make a side unit as in step 1. The unit should be 4½" square, including seam allowances. Make a set of four side units, being sure to match the orange print and the gray prints in each. Repeat to make 72 side units (18 sets of 4 matching side units).

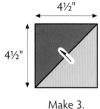

Make 72 side units,
4½" × 4½".

🍃 Fool the Eye

Blocks A, B, and C are identical except for their outer triangles. The effect is that the blocks on the outside of the quilt top will look like they are set into a dark gray border. It takes a bit of planning, but the results are worth it!

3 For one A block, gather four matching side units, four triangles from the same gray print used in the side units, three dark gray triangles, one cream triangle, and one center unit. Sew each gray triangle to a dark gray or cream triangle along the long edges. Square up to make four half-square-triangle units, each 4½" square, including seam allowances.

Make 3.   Make 1.

4 Arrange the half-square-triangle units and remaining gathered pieces from step 3 in three rows as shown. Sew together the pieces in each row, and then join the rows to make block A, which should be 12½" square, including seam allowances. Make four of block A.

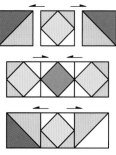

Make 4 A blocks,
12½" × 12½".

5 For one B block, gather four matching side units, four triangles from the same gray print used in the side units, two dark gray triangles, two cream triangles, and one center unit. Sew together the triangles to make half-square-triangle units as in step 3. Using the gathered pieces, repeat step 4 to make block B. Make six of block B.

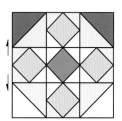

Make 6 B blocks,
12½" × 12½".

6 For one C block, gather four matching side units, four triangles from the same gray print used in the side units, four cream triangles, and one center unit. Sew together the triangles to make half-square-triangle units as in step 3. Using the gathered pieces, repeat step 4 to make block C, which should measure 12½" square, including seam allowances. Make eight of block C.

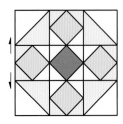

Make 8 C blocks,
12½" × 12½".

Making Blocks D and E

1 Sew together an orange and a light 2½" × 4½" rectangle to make a rectangle pair. The rectangle pair should be 4½" square, including the seam allowances. Make a set of four rectangle pairs, being sure to match the orange print and the light print in each. Repeat to make 68 (17 sets of 4 matching pairs).

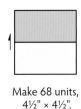

Make 68 units,
4½" × 4½".

2 For one D block, gather four matching rectangle pairs, four triangles from the same orange print used in the rectangle pairs, two dark gray triangles, two cream triangles, and one black leaf print square. Sew each orange triangle to a dark gray or cream triangle along the long edges. Square up to make four half-square-triangle units, each 4½" square, including seam allowances.

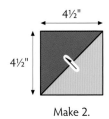

Make 2.   Make 2.

3 Arrange the half-square-triangle units and remaining gathered pieces from step 2 in three rows as shown. Sew together the pieces in each row, and then join the rows to make block D, which should be 12½" square, including seam allowances. Make 10 of block D.

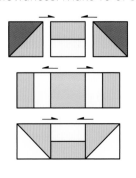
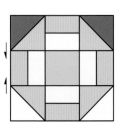

Make 10 D blocks,
12½" × 12½".

4 For one E block, gather four matching rectangle pairs, four triangles from the same orange print used in the rectangle pairs, four cream triangles, and one black leaf print square. Sew together the triangles to make half-square-triangle units as in step 2. Using the gathered pieces, repeat step 3 to make block E. Make seven of block E.

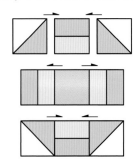
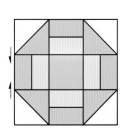

Make 7 E blocks,
12½" × 12½".

Designed and pieced by Jessica Dayon; machine quilted by David Hurd

Assembling the Quilt Top

1 Lay out the blocks in seven rows of five blocks each as shown. Sew the blocks together in each row, and then join the rows. The quilt center should be 60½" × 84½", including seam allowances.

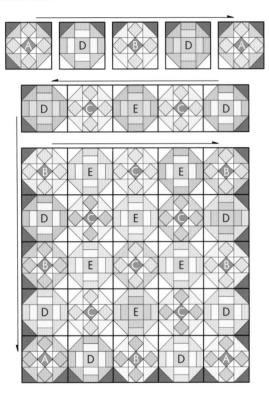

Quilt assembly

2 For the inner border, sew the dark gray 2½" × 42" strips together end to end. Trim the pieced strip to make two strips 88½" long and two strips 60½" long. Sew the 60½"-long strips to the top and bottom edges of the quilt top. Sew the 88½"-long strips to the sides. The quilt top should now be 64½" × 88½", including seam allowances.

3 For the outer border, sew the orange floral 3½" × 42" strips together end to end. Trim the pieced strip to make two strips 94½" long and two strips 64½" long. Sew the 64½"-long strips to the top and bottom edges of the quilt top. Sew the 94½"-long strips to the sides to complete the quilt top, which should measure 70½" × 94½".

Adding borders

Finishing the Quilt

For more details on any finishing steps, visit ShopMartingale.com/HowtoQuilt for free downloadable information.

1 Prepare the quilt backing so that it is about 8" larger in both directions than the quilt top.

2 Layer the quilt top, batting, and backing. Baste the layers together.

3 Hand or machine quilt as desired. The quilt shown is machine quilted with the Calder pantograph design by Natalie Gorman.

4 Using the black chevron 2½"-wide strips, make the binding and attach it to the quilt.

Icicles

When faced with the chilliest months of the year, you may end up spending more time than you want indoors. The silver lining is that you have more time to quilt! What a great opportunity to dig into your scraps and create a flurry of Dresden plates for this blue beauty. Follow the steps and you'll be skating through the process like a pro in no time.

FINISHED QUILT: 75⅜" × 75⅜"
FINISHED BLOCK: 12" × 12"

Materials

Yardage is based on 42"-wide fabric.
Fat quarters are 18" × 21".

- 13 fat quarters of assorted blue prints for appliqués and pieced setting squares and triangles

- 4¼ yards of off-white solid for blocks, pieced setting squares and triangles, and outer border

- ⅝ yard of blue floral for inner border

- ⅔ yard of navy print for binding

- 7 yards of fabric for backing*

- 84" × 84" piece of batting

- Heat-resistant template plastic (such as No-Melt Mylar Template Plastic from Dritz)

- Liquid starch or spray starch

*If your fabric is more than 42" wide after prewashing and trimming selvages, you will need only 4¾ yards of backing fabric.

Cutting

All measurements include ¼" seam allowances. Before you begin cutting, trace the circle and blade patterns on page 63 onto template plastic and cut them out. Referring to the cutting diagram below, use the blade template to cut the pieces from the fabrics indicated, rotating the template after each cut to make the best use of your fabric. You will use the circle template later in the instructions.

From the assorted blue print fat quarters, cut:
24 strips, 3⅞" × 21"; crosscut into 192 blades using the blade pattern
6 strips, 4⅛" × 21"; crosscut into 24 squares, 4⅛" × 4⅛". Cut each square into quarters diagonally to yield 4 triangles (96 total).
39 strips, 2½" × 21"; crosscut into 272 squares, 2½" × 2½"

From the off-white solid, cut:
6 strips, 12½" × 42"; crosscut into 16 squares, 12½" × 12½"
4 strips, 8½" × 42"; crosscut into 64 rectangles, 2½" × 8½"
2 strips, 4½" × 42"; crosscut into 16 squares, 4½" × 4½"
8 strips, 2½" × 42"

From the blue floral, cut:
8 strips, 2" × 42"

From the navy print, cut:
8 strips, 2½" × 42"

Cutting diagram

Making the Dresden Plate Blocks

Use a ¼" seam allowance. Press all seam allowances in the direction indicated by the arrows.

 Fold a blue blade in half widthwise, with right sides together. Sew along the top edge, backstitching at the beginning and end. Trim the top edge to ⅛" from the seamline. Holding the seams open, turn the blade right side out and press flat. Repeat to prepare 192 blades.

Make 192 units.

 Sew 12 blades together to form a Dresden plate. Repeat to make 16 Dresden units.

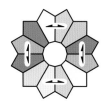

Make 16 units.

 Place the circle template on an off-white 4½" square and trace around it, adding a ½" seam allowance. Cut out on the drawn line. Use a basting stitch (machine-stitch length of about 5) to sew around the edge of the fabric circle, leaving long thread ends. Position the circle template in the center of the basted fabric circle and gather the threads around it. Saturate the seam allowance with starch and press from the wrong side; work on a little section of the edge at a time, gliding the iron from the outside of the circle over the cinched fabric toward the inside. Let dry completely. Trim off the excess seam allowance, leaving a ¼" seam allowance. Repeat to cut and prepare 16 Dresden center circles.

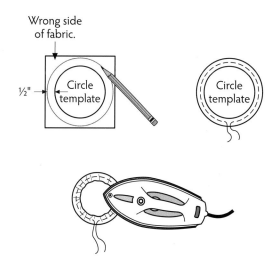

 Machine or hand appliqué a Dresden plate to an off-white 12½" square. Then machine or hand appliqué a prepared center circle to the center to make a block. Make 16 Dresden plate blocks, each 12½" square, including seam allowances.

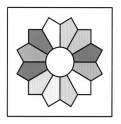

Make 16 blocks, 12½" × 12½".

❄ Spinning Plates

To speed things up, work assembly-line efficiency into the process by chain piecing your Dresden units. In step 1 above, fold several blades in half and stitch them along the wide folded edge one after the other, without stopping to cut the threads. When you've finished your chain, snip the threads between blades to separate them. Take a similar approach in step 2 by chain piecing blades into pairs and then into trios and then again when joining the blade trios to make circular units.

② Referring to the diagram, lay out four assorted blue 2½" squares, four off-white 2½" × 8½" rectangles, and one 16-patch unit in three rows. Sew the pieces together in each row, and then join the rows to make a setting square, which should be 12½" square, including seam allowances. Make nine setting squares.

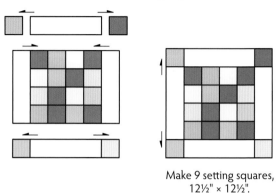

Make 9 setting squares,
12½" × 12½".

③ Lay out six assorted blue 2½" squares and four assorted blue triangles in four rows. Sew the pieces together in each row. Sew the rows together to make a large pieced triangle. Make 12 large pieced triangles.

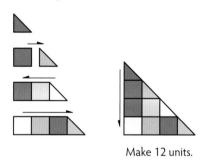

Make 12 units.

④ Referring to the diagram, lay out two assorted blue print triangles, two off-white 2½" × 8½" rectangles, one blue print 2½" square, and one pieced large triangle in three rows. Sew the pieces

Making the Setting Squares and Triangles

① Lay out 16 assorted blue 2½" squares in four rows of four squares each. Sew the squares together in each row. Sew the rows together to make a 16-patch unit. The unit should be 8½" square, including seam allowances. Make nine 16-patch units.

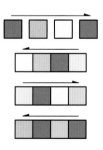

Make 9 units,
8½" × 8½".

❄ ❄ ❄ ❄ ❄

Designed and pieced by Jessica Dayon; quilted by David Hurd

together in each row, and then join the rows to make a side setting triangle. Make 12 side setting triangles.

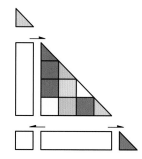

Make 12 units.

⑤ Lay out four assorted blue triangles and two assorted blue 2½" squares in two horizontal rows as shown. Sew the pieces into rows. Join the rows to make a small pieced triangle. Make four small pieced triangles.

Make 4 units.

6 Referring to the diagram, sew together two assorted blue print triangles and one off-white 2½" × 8½" rectangle in a row. Sew to the bottom edge of a small pieced triangle to make a corner setting triangle. Make four corner setting triangles.

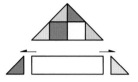

Make 4 units.

Assembling the Quilt Top

1 Referring to the quilt assembly diagram, lay out the blocks, setting squares, and side setting triangles in seven diagonal rows. Sew the pieces together in each row, and then join the rows. Add the corner setting triangles to complete the quilt center. The quilt center should be 68⅜" square, including seam allowances.

Quilt assembly

2 For the inner border, sew two blue floral 2" × 42" strips together end to end. Repeat to make four pieced strips. Trim two strips to 68⅜" long. Sew these strips to the sides of the quilt top. Trim the remaining two pieced strips to 71⅜" long. Sew these strips to the top and bottom edges. The quilt top should now be 71⅜" square, including seam allowances.

3 For the outer border, sew two off-white 2½" × 42" strips together end to end. Repeat to make four pieced strips. Trim two strips to 71⅜" long. Sew these strips to the sides of the quilt top. Trim the remaining two pieced strips to 75⅜" long. Sew these strips to the top and bottom edges to complete the quilt top, which should measure 75⅜" square.

Adding borders

Finishing the Quilt

For more details on any finishing steps, visit ShopMartingale.com/HowtoQuilt for free downloadable information.

1 Prepare the quilt backing so that it is about 8" larger in both directions than the quilt top.

2 Layer the quilt top, batting, and backing. Baste the layers together.

3 Hand or machine quilt as desired. The quilt shown is quilted with the Flamingo Sunset pantograph design from Anne Bright Designs.

4 Using the navy 2½"-wide strips, make the binding and attach it to the quilt.

The blade pattern includes seam allowances.

The circle pattern does not include seam allowances.

Circle
Cut 16 from off-white solid.

Blade
Cut 192 from assorted blue prints.

Tradition

Pine trees and stars are the perfect backdrop for the season. Hang this festive quilt anywhere you need a little cheer, or use it as a table covering under a holiday display.

FINISHED QUILT: 59½" × 59½"
FINISHED BLOCK: 10" × 10"

Materials

Yardage is based on 42"-wide fabric.
Fat quarters are 18" × 21".

- 4 fat quarters (lime, pear, fern, and checked green) for blocks
- 3 fat quarters (red dot, coral geometric, and coral floral) for blocks
- 2½ yards of ivory solid for background
- 1 fat quarter of cream print for blocks
- ½ yard of textured green for big trees
- ¼ yard of green dot for small trees
- ¼ yard of taupe print for Tree blocks
- ¼ yard of jade print for border 1
- ⅜ yard of coral dot for border 3
- ⅞ yard of green floral for border 4
- ⅝ yard of salmon print for binding
- 3⅔ yards of fabric for backing
- 66" × 66" piece of batting
- Template plastic or stiff paper

Cutting

All measurements include ¼" seam allowances. Before you begin cutting, trace the patterns on pages 72 and 73 onto template plastic or other template-making material and cut them out. Use the templates to cut the pieces from the fabrics indicated. When cutting pieces, rotate every other piece 180° to make the best use of your fabric.

From the lime green fat quarter, cut:
1 square, 6¼" × 6¼"

From the pear green fat quarter, cut:
3 strips, 1¾" × 21"; crosscut into 32 squares, 1¾" × 1¾"

From the fern green fat quarter, cut:
2 strips, 5½" × 21"; crosscut into 4 squares, 5½" × 5½"

From the checked green fat quarter, cut:
4 strips, 3⅜" × 21"; crosscut into 16 squares, 3⅜" × 3⅜"

From the red dot fat quarter, cut *in the following order:*
3 strips, 2⅞" × 21"; crosscut into 16 squares, 2⅞" × 2⅞"
1 square, 6¼" × 6¼"
2 strips, 3½" × 14¾"; crosscut into 8 squares, 3½" × 3½"

From the coral geometric fat quarter, cut:
1 strip, 3" × 21"; crosscut into 4 squares, 3" × 3"

From the coral floral fat quarter, cut:
4 strips, 3⅜" × 21"; crosscut into 16 squares, 3⅜" × 3⅜"

Continued on page 66

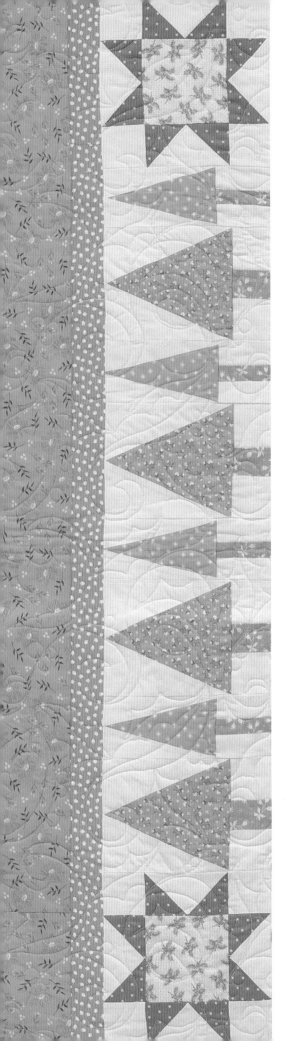

Continued from page 65

From the ivory solid, cut:
2 strips, 6½" × 42"; crosscut into:
    16 big-tree backgrounds
    16 big-tree backgrounds reversed
2 strips, 6¼" × 42"; crosscut into 8 squares, 6¼" × 6¼"
1 strip, 5⅞" × 42; crosscut into:
    16 small-tree backgrounds
    16 small-tree backgrounds reversed
1 strip, 5¼" × 42"; crosscut into 4 squares, 5¼" × 5¼"
2 strips, 3½" × 42"; crosscut into 16 squares, 3½" × 3½"
1 strip, 3⅜" × 42"; crosscut into 8 squares, 3⅜" × 3⅜"
2 strips, 3⅛" × 42"; crosscut into 32 rectangles, 1½" × 3⅛"
3 strips, 3" × 42"; crosscut into:
    16 squares, 3" × 3"
    16 rectangles, 1¾" × 3"
3 strips, 2½" × 42"; crosscut into 48 squares, 2½" × 2½"
1 strip, 1¾" × 42"; crosscut into 16 squares, 1¾" × 1¾"

From the cream print, cut:
1 strip, 4½" × 21"; crosscut into 4 squares, 4½" × 4½"
2 strips, 3½" × 21"; crosscut into 8 squares, 3½" × 3½"

From the textured green, cut:
2 strips, 6½" × 42"; crosscut into 16 big trees

From the green dot, cut:
1 strip, 5⅞" × 42"; crosscut into 16 small trees

From the taupe print, cut:
1 strip, 3⅛" × 42"; crosscut into 16 rectangles, 1¼" × 3⅛"
1 strip, 2½" × 42"; crosscut into 16 rectangles, 1¾" × 2½"

From the jade print for border 1, cut:
4 strips, 1½" × 42"; crosscut into:
    2 strips, 1½" × 32½"
    2 strips, 1½" × 30½"

From the coral dot for border 3, cut:
6 strips, 2" × 42"

From the green floral for border 4, cut:
6 strips, 4½" × 42"

From the salmon print for binding, cut:
7 strips, 2½" × 42"

Making the Goose Chase Block

Use a ¼" seam allowance. Press all seam allowances in the direction indicated by the arrows.

1 Using the lime 6¼" square and four ivory 3⅜" squares, refer to step 1 of "Making the Blocks" on page 14 to make four flying-geese units. Each unit should be 3" × 5½", including seam allowances.

Make 4 units,
3" × 5½".

2 Using red dot instead of lime, repeat step 1 to make four flying-geese units.

Make 4 units,
3" × 5½".

3 Join a green and a red flying-geese unit to make a flying-geese pair. Make four units, each 5½" square, including seam allowances.

Make 4 units,
5½" × 5½".

4 Lay out the flying-geese pairs in two rows as shown. Sew the pieces in each row together, and then join the rows to make a Goose Chase block. The block should be 10½" square, including seam allowances.

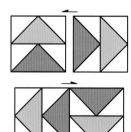
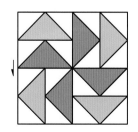

Make 1 block,
10½" × 10½".

Making the Double Star Blocks

1 Draw a diagonal line from corner to corner on the wrong side of two pear green 1¾" squares. Align a square at one end of an ivory 1¾" × 3" rectangle, right sides together, with the line positioned as shown. Sew on the line. Trim, leaving a ¼" seam allowance. Press. Repeat to add the second marked square to the other end of the rectangle. Make 16 pear green flying-geese units measuring 1¾" × 3".

Make 16 units,
1¾" × 3".

2 Sew four ivory 1¾" squares, four pear green flying-geese units, and one coral geometric 3" square together in three rows as shown. Join the rows to make a small star unit. The unit should be 5½" square, including seam allowances. Repeat to make four small star units.

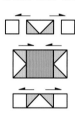

Make 4 units,
5½" × 5½".

3 Using an ivory 6¼" square and four coral floral 3⅜" squares, refer again to step 1 of "Making the Blocks" to make four flying-geese units. Each unit should be 3" × 5½", including seam allowances. Make 16 flying-geese units.

Make 16 units,
3" × 5½".

and a small star unit into three horizontal rows as shown. Sew the pieces in each row together, and then join the rows to make a Double Star block. The block should be 10½" square, including seam allowances. Repeat to make four Double Star blocks.

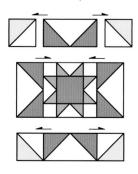
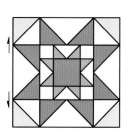

Make 4 blocks,
10½" × 10½".

Making the Star Blocks

1 Draw a diagonal line from corner to corner on the wrong side of four ivory 3" squares. Align one 3" square, right sides together, with a corner of a fern green 5½" square. Sew on the diagonal line. Cut ¼" from the stitching line. Press. Repeat with the other squares at the remaining corners to make a block-center unit. Make four units, each 5½" square, including seam allowances.

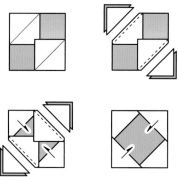

Make 4 units,
5½" × 5½".

2 Draw a diagonal line from corner to corner on the wrong side of an ivory 3½" square. Place it, right sides together, on a red dot 3½" square and sew ¼" from both sides of the marked line. Cut on the line and press. Using a square ruler, line up the 45° line with the diagonal of the half-square-triangle

4 Draw a diagonal line from corner to corner on the wrong side of an ivory 3½" square. Place it, right sides together, on a 3½" cream print square and sew ¼" from both sides of the marked line. Cut on the line and press. Using a square ruler, line up the 45° line with the diagonal of the half-square-triangle unit and trim the unit to 3" square. Repeat with the remaining unit. Make 16 half-square-triangle units.

Make 16 units.

5 Arrange four half-square-triangle units from step 4, four flying-geese units from step 3,

unit and trim the unit to 3" square. Repeat with the remaining unit. Make 16 half-square-triangle units.

Make 16 units.

3 Using an ivory 6¼" square and four checked green 3⅜" squares, refer again to step 1 of "Making the Blocks" to make four flying-geese units. Each unit should be 3" × 5½", including seam allowances. Make 16 flying-geese units.

Make 16 units,
3" × 5½".

4 Arrange four half-square-triangle units from step 2, four flying-geese units from step 3, and a block center into three horizontal rows as shown. Sew the pieces in each row together, and then join the rows to make a Star block. The block should be 10½" square, including seam allowances. Repeat to make four Star blocks.

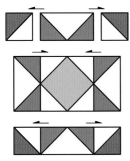

Make 4 blocks,
10½" × 10½".

5 Using an ivory 5¼" square and four red A 2⅞" squares, refer again to step 1 of "Making the Blocks" to make four flying-geese units. Each unit should be 2½" × 4½", including seam allowances. Make 16 flying-geese units.

Make 16 units,
2½" × 4½".

6 Arrange four flying-geese units from step 5, four ivory 2½" squares, and one cream 4½" square into three horizontal rows as shown. Sew the pieces in each row together, and then join the rows to make a border Star block. The block should be 8½" square, including seam allowances. Repeat to make four border Star blocks.

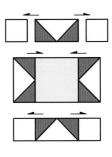

Make 4 blocks,
8½" × 8½".

Making the Tree Blocks

1 Sew together one textured green big tree and one each of ivory big-tree background and big-tree background reversed triangles to make a big treetop. The treetop should be 5¾" × 6½", including seam allowances. Make 16 big treetop units.

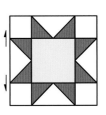

Make 16 units,
5¾" × 6½".

2 Sew together two ivory 2½" squares and one taupe 1¾" × 2½" rectangle as shown to make a big trunk unit. The unit should be 2½" × 5¾", including seam allowances. Make 16.

Make 16 units,
2½" × 5¾".

3 Join a big treetop and a big trunk unit to make a big Tree block. The block should be 5¾" × 8½", including seam allowances. Make 16 big Tree blocks.

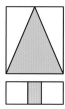 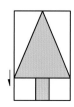

Make 16 blocks,
5¾" × 8½".

4 Sew together one green dot small tree and one each of ivory small-tree background and small-tree background reversed triangles to make a small treetop. The treetop should be 3¼" × 5⅞", including seam allowances. Make 16.

Make 16 units,
3¼" × 5⅞".

5 Sew together two ivory 1½" × 3⅛" rectangles and one taupe 1¼" × 3⅛" rectangle as shown to make a small trunk unit. The unit should be 3¼" × 3⅛", including seam allowances. Make 16.

Make 16 units,
3¼" × 3⅛".

6 Join a small treetop and small trunk unit to make a small Tree block. The block should be 3¼" × 8½", including seam allowances. Make 16.

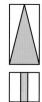 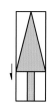

Make 16 blocks,
3¼" × 8½".

Assembling the Quilt Top

1 Lay out the Double Star blocks, Star blocks, and Goose Chase block in three rows of three blocks each as shown in the quilt assembly diagram. Sew together the blocks in each row, and then join the rows to make the quilt center, which should be 30½" square, including seam allowances.

Quilt assembly

2 Sew four big Tree blocks and four small Tree blocks together to make a short tree border. The border should be 8½" × 32½", including seam allowances. Make two short tree borders.

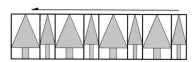

Make 2 borders. 8½" × 32½".

3 Sew two border Star blocks, four big Tree blocks, and four small Tree blocks together to make a long tree border. The border should be 8½" × 48½", including seam allowances. Make two long tree borders.

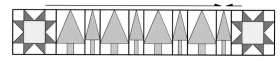

Make 2 borders, 8½" × 48½".

✳ ✳ ✳ ✳ ✳ ✳

Designed and pieced by Jessica Dayon; quilted by David Hurd

4 Sew the jade print 1½" × 30½" strips to the sides of the quilt top. Sew the jade print 1½" × 32½" strips to the top and bottom edges of the quilt top. The quilt top should now be 32½" square, including seam allowances.

5 Sew the short tree borders to the sides of the quilt top. Sew the long tree borders to the top and bottom edges of the quilt top. The quilt top should now be 48½" square, including seam allowances.

6 For the third border, sew the coral dot 2" × 42" strips together end to end. From the pieced strip, cut two strips 51½" long and two strips 48½" long. Sew the 48½"-long strips to the sides of the quilt top. Sew the 51½"-long strips to the top and bottom edges of the quilt top. The quilt top should now be 51½" square, including seam allowances.

7 For the fourth border, sew the green floral 4½" × 42" strips together end to end. From the pieced strip, cut two strips 59½" long and two strips 51½" long. Sew the 51½"-long strips to the sides of the quilt top. Sew the 59½"-long strips to the top and bottom edges to complete the quilt top, which should measure 59½" square.

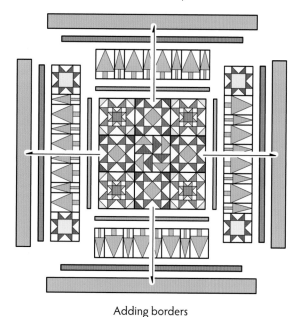

Adding borders

Finishing the Quilt

For more details on any finishing steps, visit ShopMartingale.com/HowtoQuilt for free downloadable information.

1 Prepare the quilt backing so that it is about 6" larger in both directions than the quilt top.

2 Layer the quilt top, batting, and backing. Baste the layers together.

3 Hand or machine quilt as desired. The quilt shown is quilted with the Holly Berries pantograph design from Anne Bright Designs.

4 Using the salmon print 2½"-wide strips, make the binding and attach it to the quilt.

Templates include seam allowances.

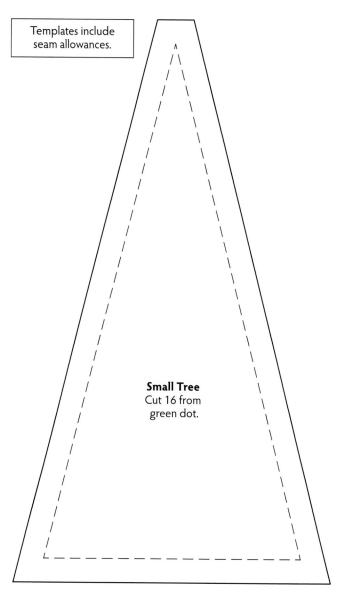

Small Tree
Cut 16 from
green dot.

❄

Spruce It Up

If you're feeling extra festive, consider festooning your trees with decorations. Zigzag across each tree as you quilt to suggest garlands or strings of lights, and then stitch a shining star at the tippy top. For handwork enthusiasts, add shiny beads or colorful buttons to suggest ornaments. Love embroidery? Work a few of your favorite stitches to mimic branches, perch birds, dot poinsettias, or hang baubles. Explore the ribbons, specialty threads, and embellishments in your stash, and see what might light up your forest border!

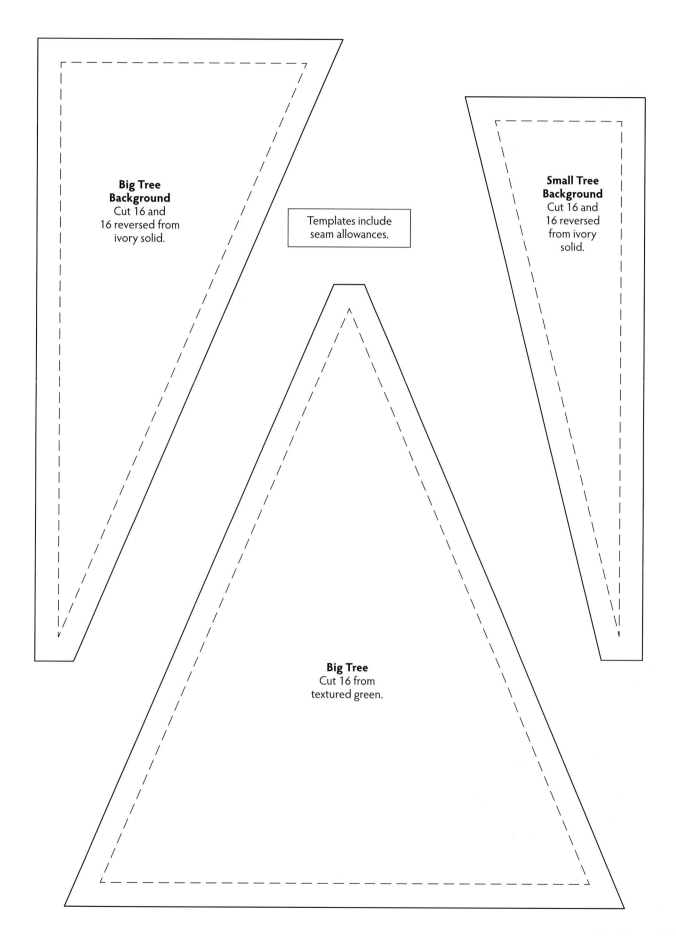

Big Tree Background
Cut 16 and 16 reversed from ivory solid.

Templates include seam allowances.

Small Tree Background
Cut 16 and 16 reversed from ivory solid.

Big Tree
Cut 16 from textured green.

Ribbons

Jack Frost and Old Man Winter might as well face the cold, hard truth: a handmade quilt is full of love and warmth that they'll never be able to penetrate. So bring on the snow, the winds, and the ice—you're covered.

FINISHED QUILT: 92½" × 92½"
FINISHED BLOCK: 16" × 16"

Materials

Yardage is based on 42"-wide fabric.

- 3⅝ yards of white solid for blocks
- ⅔ yard of dark gray print for blocks
- 2 yards of aqua dot for blocks
- 3 yards of red print for blocks and binding
- 1⅛ yards of light gray gingham for blocks
- 1 yard of light gray print for inner border
- 1⅛ yards of red stripe for outer border
- 8½ yards of fabric for backing
- 101" × 101" piece of batting

Cutting

All measurements include ¼" seam allowances.

From the white solid, cut:
15 strips, 5½" × 42"; crosscut into 100 squares, 5½" × 5½".
  Cut the squares into quarters diagonally to yield 4 triangles (400 total).
7 strips, 5" × 42"; crosscut into 50 squares, 5" × 5"

From the dark gray print, cut:
4 strips, 5" × 42"; crosscut into 25 squares, 5" × 5"

From the aqua dot, cut:
8 strips, 5½" × 42"; crosscut into 50 squares, 5½" × 5½".
  Cut the squares into quarters diagonally to yield 4 triangles (200 total).
4 strips, 5" × 42"; crosscut into 25 squares, 5" × 5"

From the red print, cut:
2 strips, 5½" × 42"; crosscut into 10 squares, 5½" × 5½".
  Cut the squares into quarters diagonally to yield 4 triangles (40 total).
13 strips, 4½" × 42"; crosscut into 100 squares, 4½" × 4½"
10 strips, 2½" × 42"

From the light gray gingham, cut:
6 strips, 5½" × 42"; crosscut into 40 squares, 5½" × 5½".
  Cut the squares into quarters diagonally to yield 4 triangles (160 total).

Continued on page 76

Continued from page 75

From the light gray print, cut:

9 strips, 3½" × 42"

From the red stripe, cut:

10 strips, 3½" × 42"

Making the Blocks

Use a ¼" seam allowance. Press all seam allowances in the direction indicated by the arrows.

1 Draw a diagonal line from corner to corner on the wrong side of a white 5" square. Place the marked square, right sides together, on a 5" dark gray square; sew ¼" from both sides of the line. Cut on the line and press. Trim to 4½" square. Repeat with the remaining unit. Make 50 gray half-square-triangle units.

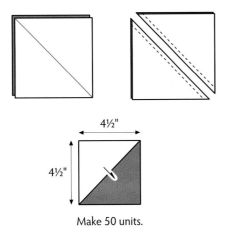

Make 50 units.

2 Using an aqua dot and a white 5" square, make two half-square-triangle units as in step 1. Trim each to 4½" square, including seam allowances. Repeat to make 50 aqua half-square-triangle units.

Make 50 units.

3 Join one red and one white triangle along short edges; then join one aqua dot and one white triangle. Join the pairs to make a quarter-square-triangle unit. Align the 45° line of a ruler on a diagonal seam and the center point of the unit with the 2¼" ruler measurements. Trim. Rotate the unit 180°. Align the left and bottom edges of the unit with the 4½" lines of the ruler. Trim to 4½" square, including seam allowances. Repeat to make 40 quarter-square-triangle units.

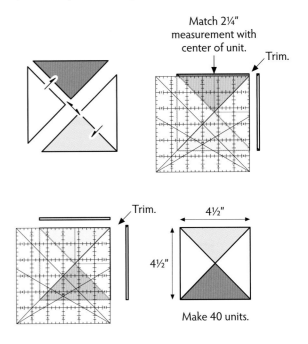

Match 2¼" measurement with center of unit.

Trim.

Trim.

4½"

4½"

Make 40 units.

4 Using gray gingham, aqua dot, and white triangles, make 4½" quarter-square-triangle units as in step 3. Make 160 units.

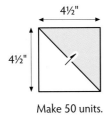

4½"

4½"

Make 160 units.

5 Gather two gray half-square-triangle units, two aqua half-square-triangle units, four red/aqua quarter-square-triangle units, four gray gingham/aqua quarter-square-triangle units, and four red 4½" squares. Sew into four rows as shown on page 77, paying close attention to the direction of

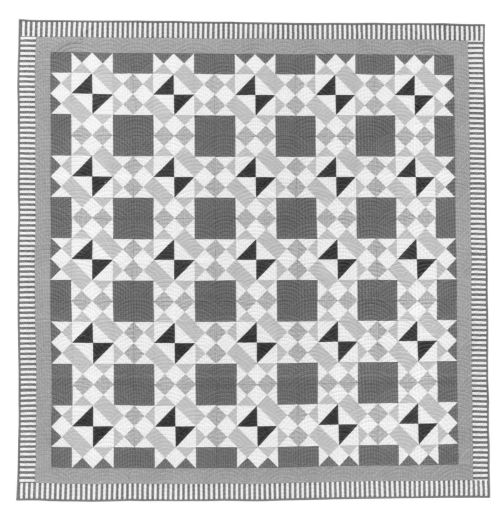

Designed and pieced by Jessica Dayon; machine quilted by Kaitlyn Howell

the center half-square-triangle units. Join the rows to make block A, which should be 16½" square, including seam allowances. Make two of block A.

6 Using the same pieces as in step 5, but with a different orientation of the half-square-triangle units in the center, make two of block B.

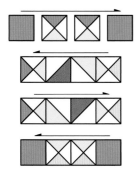

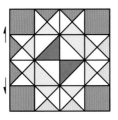

Make 2 A blocks,
16½" × 16½".

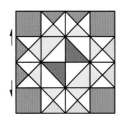

Make 2 B blocks,
16½" × 16½".

8 Using the same pieces as in step 7, but with a different orientation of the half-square-triangle units in the center, make six of block D.

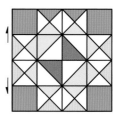

Make 6 D blocks,
16½" × 16½".

9 For an E block, gather two gray half-square-triangle units, two aqua half-square-triangle units, eight gray gingham/aqua quarter-square-triangle units from step 4, and four red A 4½" squares. Assemble the pieces into four horizontal rows as shown. Pay close attention to the direction of the center half-square-triangle units. Sew the pieces in each row together, and then join the rows to make block E. The block should be 16½" square, including seam allowances. Make nine of block E.

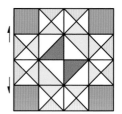

Make 9 E blocks,
16½" × 16½".

Assembling the Quilt Top

1 Lay out blocks A–E in five rows of five blocks each as shown in the quilt assembly diagram on page 79. Sew together the blocks in each row, and then join the rows to make the quilt center. The quilt center should be 80½" square, including seam allowances.

2 For the inner border, sew the light gray 3½" × 42" strips together end to end. From the pieced strip, cut two strips 86½" long and two strips 80½" long. Sew the 80½"-long strips to the

7 For a C block, gather two gray half-square-triangle units, two aqua half-square-triangle units, two red/aqua quarter-square-triangle units, six gray gingham/aqua quarter-square triangles from step 4, and four red 4½" squares. Assemble the pieces into four horizontal rows as shown. Pay close attention to the direction of the center half-square-triangle units. Sew the pieces in each row together, and then join the rows to make block C. The block should be 16½" square, including seam allowances. Make six of block C.

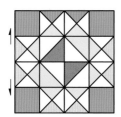

Make 6 C blocks,
16½" × 16½".

sides of the quilt center. Sew the 86½"-long strips to the top and bottom edges. The quilt top should now be 86½" square, including seam allowances.

3 For the outer border, sew the red stripe 3½" × 42" strips together end to end. From the pieced strip, cut two strips 92½" long and two strips 86½" long. Sew the 86½"-long strips to the sides of the quilt top. Sew the 92½"-long strips to the top and bottom edges to complete the quilt top, which should measure 92½" square.

Finishing the Quilt

For more details on any finishing steps, visit ShopMartingale.com/HowtoQuilt for free downloadable information.

1 Prepare the quilt backing so that it is about 8" larger in both directions than the quilt top.

2 Layer the quilt top, batting, and backing. Baste the layers together.

3 Hand or machine quilt as desired. The quilt shown is quilted with the Baptist Fan E2E pantograph design from Mountaintop Quilting.

4 Using the red 2½"-wide strips, make the binding and attach it to the quilt.

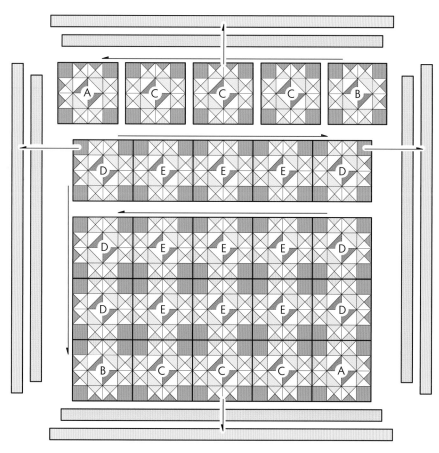

Quilt assembly

Acknowledgments

I'm grateful to:

• My children—Isabelle, Evy, Poppy, and Ben. Thank you for folding fabric, sorting scraps, giving opinions, and gathering around my sewing machine to play while I sewed these quilts. You never tired of the hum of my sewing machine and loved sitting with me while I spent time creating. Your presence has brought me so much joy. I'll love each one of you every single day of forever.

• Mom, Bern, Bernie, Hope, Sharon, Eric, Maddie, Callie, Avery, Grandma and Grandpa Everett, Dad, Leticia, TJ, Cindy, Lexi, Livvie, Grandma and Grandpa Hughes, Nana and Poppy, Jeanne, Leeann, Vicky, and Cheryl—for always encouraging me!

• Martingale, for believing in my ideas and allowing me to bring these patterns to life in a book. Laurie, for your help and for always answering my emails quickly. Beth, for always being available for questions.

• Moda Fabrics, for providing fabric for the quilts in this book. I could use your fabrics every day forever and never tire of them. Lissa Alexander, for talking with me the first time in 2017 and for every email since then. Thank you for being so encouraging, supportive, and generous! You have genuinely made an impact on my life.

• Riley Blake Fabrics, for providing fabrics for quilts in this book. I love the lines that you print and I'm honored to be able to work with them! Your basics are amazing! Lacie, for being so amazingly quick at email response and for always being so generous.

• Baby Lock, for loaning me an Aria sewing machine to sew these quilts. I enjoyed every second of sewing on it!

• Quilters David Hurd, Teresa Silva, and Kaitlyn Howell. You made my quilt tops shine and I'm so grateful for your hard work. David, a special thank you for always working so fast on everything I send you!

About the Author

Jessica Dayon is a self-taught quilter who fell in love with quilting from the first day she started. She has been quilting every day since. She shares quilting patterns and tutorials on her blog at jessicadayon.blogspot.com.

Her designs have been featured by the Moda Bake Shop as well as in magazines including *Quilting, American Patchwork & Quilting*, and *McCall's Quilting*.

Jessica is a stay-at-home wife and mother of four young children. In addition to quilting, her hobbies are cross-stitch, embroidery, crochet, hand sewing, cooking, and gardening.

You can find Jessica on her blog and also on Instagram at @jessicadayon, where she shares her daily work, current projects, inspiration, and pattern news.